# Who Will Be My Teacher?

# Who Will Be My Teacher?

## Marjory Goldfinch Ward

Fleming H. Revell
A Division of Baker Book House
Grand Rapids, Michigan 49516

Unless otherwise identified, Scripture quotations in this book are from the Holy Bible, New International Version, copyright © 1973, 1978, 1984 International Bible Society. Used by permission of Zondervan Bible Publishers.

Scripture quotations identified NEB are from The New English Bible. Copyright © The Delegates of the Oxford University Press and the Syndics of the Cambridge University Press 1961, 1970. Reprinted by permission.

Scripture quotations identified NAS are from the New American Standard Bible, © The Lockman Foundation 1960, 1962, 1963, 1968, 1971, 1972, 1973, 1975, 1977.

Scripture quotations identified RSV are from the Revised Standard Version of the Bible, copyrighted © 1946, 1952, 1971, by the Division of Christian Education of the National Council of the Churches of Christ in the United States of America, and are used by permission. All rights reserved.

Scripture verses marked TLB are taken from The Living Bible, Copyright © 1971. Used by permission of Tyndale House Publishers, Inc., Wheaton, IL 60189. All right reserved.

Scripture quotations identified WEYMOUTH are from WEYMOUTH'S NEW TESTAMENT IN MODERN SPEECH by Richard Francis Weymouth. Published by special arrangement with James Clarke & Company, Ltd., and reprinted by permission of Harper & Row, Publishers, Inc.

Excerpts from DAILY WITH THE KING, by W. Glyn Evans are Copyright © 1979. Moody Bible Institute of Chicago. Moody Press. Used by permission.

Material from *Edges of His Ways* by Amy Carmichael, copyright © 1955 Dohnavur Fellowship (Ft. Washington, PA: Christian Literature Crusade; London: S.P.C.K.). Used by permission.

Excerpt from *If Jesus Came to My House* by Joan Gale Thomas is copyright © Lothrop, Lee and Shepard. Reprinted by permission of William Morrow and Company, Inc.

Library of Congress Cataloging-in-Publication Data

Ward, Marjory G. (Marjory Goldfinch)
    Who will be my teacher? : affirming devotions for teachers / Marjory Goldfinch Ward.
        p.   cm.
    ISBN 0-8007-1654-X
    1. Teachers—Prayer-books and devotions—English.
BV4596.T43W37   1991
242'.68—dc20                                                    91-9649
                                                                    CIP

Copyright © 1991 by Marjory Goldfinch Ward
Published by Fleming H. Revell
a division of Baker Book House Company
P.O. Box 6287, Grand Rapids, MI 49516-6287

Second printing, January 1993

*Printed in the United States of America*

To every teacher I ever had,
and that includes every person I ever taught,
for each of them has been my teacher.

# Contents

## December

## January

## February

## March

## April

Contents

# Introduction

Shortly after our first child went to college and our youngest child entered first grade I also returned to school—as a teacher. My first lesson was simple: I found out how much I had to learn.

I quickly found my teachers. My first group of ninth-grade students taught me that not all answers can be found in textbooks. They accepted me and helped me adjust to a new role, a new way of life.

The other teachers made me feel at home. They let me know that it is normal to feel overwhelmed by an impossible task.

The school principal became my mentor in public education. His integrity and fierce concern for students set priorities for me as an educator.

From that first experience I have watched and learned from other teachers. I have noticed how eager we are to learn from one another. We crave opportunities to share ideas. We dread and avoid situations that bore and stifle us. And we keep on learning.

We mark our lives by the school bell. The freshness of beginning the school year flows swiftly into seasonal holidays, which break the rhythm of the days and weeks. Each season brings out, especially in the elementary schools, eye-catching displays that signal the swift passing of that school year.

After twenty years of "teacher watching," each time I walk into a school I take fresh delight in seeing teachers do what they do best: actively moving among their students or standing before them with a quiet intensity that commands attention, giving all their energy to the task, and going home exhausted or exhilarated, depending on the response that they have received that day. Teachers face incredible challenges and most of them do not give up.

I have written from the experiences of these other teachers as well as from my own. There is one excerpt for each of the eighteen weeks of a school semester, divided into the months that include the delightful seasonal emphases marking special holidays. There are affirmations also for "time out," when teachers and students get away from each other to rest and renew their energy.

As students grow up and leave us, graduating before we think it possible, others take their places. Occasionally one will come back to say, "Thank you. You made a difference."

To every teacher I would like to say in this book:

"Thank you. You make a difference."

Marjory Ward
Columbia, South Carolina

# Who Will Be My Teacher?

# Who Will Be My Teacher?
## Isaiah 30:18–21

Yesterday I went by the school and saw the children crowding around the doors to look at the class lists posted on the window and asking each other eagerly,

"Who's your teacher?"

"Oh, no! Who's mine?"

"All *right!*"

I began to ask myself, *Who's* my *teacher this year?*

The longer I teach, the more clearly I realize that I need someone to teach *me*.

My students will look to me as "the expert" (or they won't, which may be worse). But— who will be *my* teacher?

Isaiah said that the one who teaches me will not be hidden out of sight, but with my own eyes I shall see him all the time.

Does that mean *You*, Lord? Are You my teacher?

The prophet also said that You yearn to be gracious to me, and that You rise quickly to show me compassion.

My students may not realize it, but I really want to be gracious to them. In my "exalted" position of authority over them I want to respond quickly to their need for help. But I know that they will try my patience, and I may have to give them a little of the "bread of adversity and the water of affliction." I know that correction and positive discipline are for their own good and for the security of the class, but they can't always see that.

When it comes to Your teaching *me*, I don't always see it, either, Lord. I would rather be "carried to the skies on flowery beds of ease," as the old hymn says. I'd rather have perfect pupils, easy curriculum, an immaculate classroom, saintly colleagues, and permissive administrators who spend most of their time congratulating me. I don't like this "bread of adversity" idea.

Like my students, I also have to learn the hard way. You're patient with me while I learn, even though I know I try Your patience, too.

Thank You for Your patience.
Thank You for Your mercy.
Thank You even for the tough times.
Thank You for correcting me when I
need it.
Thank You for being my Teacher this year.

I will instruct you and teach you
in the way you should go;
I will counsel you and watch
over you.
. . . the Lord's unfailing love
surrounds the man who trusts in
him.
                    Psalm 32:8, 10

# "What Is That Among So Many?"
## John 6:9–13

A little boy brought his lunch that day. Andrew and the other disciples found that little lunch as they looked around for possible ways to feed a crowd of thousands of people. They even brought this ridiculously inadequate supply of food to Jesus. Did that little boy give up his lunch voluntarily? I wonder.

Five little rolls and two small fish made a good lunch for a small boy but a puny offering for the Master, who needed to feed a multitude.

Sometimes I feel coerced into giving what little I have to this "multitude" in front of me. These students need so much from me; I wonder if I'll have anything left when they get through. They need *everything:* all the knowledge I can get together, the skills I contrive, and most of all, my patient understanding and accepting love. I know that some of them have no stability in their lives. Their homes add pressure and tension, and they come to school desperately vulnerable.

What do I have among so many?

In her book *Edges of His Ways*, Amy Carmichael said:

> I hoped to do so much, and I have done nothing worth bringing to Thee—that is how we feel. The story of the five thousand describes "broken pieces" . . . yet of those fragments our Lord said, "Gather them up" . . . Our dear Lord cares for the broken pieces of our lives, the fragments of all we meant to do, the little that we have to gather up and offer, and He will use even these fragments. He will not let even the least of our little broken things be lost.

I give You what I do have, Lord,
I know it's not much.
I give it to You, because You can do wonders
with it.
My "tiny lunch" can become bits and pieces
that my students need:

a little patience,
a little understanding,
some knowledge,
a few skills—
and You meet the need.
Only You can see that there is enough,
and a lot left over.

They all ate to their hearts' content; and
twelve great basketfuls of scraps were
picked up. . . .

Mark 6:42, 43 NEB

# What Will *I* Have Left?
# Matthew 14:13–21

You tried to get away from the crowds, Lord.
They followed You, persistently clamoring for
more.
You gave them what they needed.
What was left for You?
When they all left, did You get away to be
alone?
Did You ever have the chance to grieve
privately for John?

When I have given out everything I have all
day,
When I get home, drained and tired,
I need to be alone.
I need to think through my day.
Sometimes I need to mourn losses or regret
failures.

With all this giving out, Lord,
What will I have left for my family?
What will I have left for myself?


How can I care about individuals all day?
How can I pay attention to the endless
details?
How can I keep up with all I have to do?
How can I manage a classroom?
How can I teach?
How can I respond patiently and consistently,
And have anything at all left at the end of the
day?


My children need my patient caring.
My husband needs my attention.
My household needs my time.
I'm tired of dust and clutter,
Of corners unattended
And laundry piled up.


I'm tired, period, Lord,
When I get home at the end of the day.


What about *me*, Lord, what about me?

They who wait for the Lord shall renew
their strength,
they shall mount up with wings like
eagles,
they shall run and not be weary,
they shall walk and not faint.

Isaiah 40:31 RSV

I wait on You, Lord.
I am still and quiet for this little space of time.
I am waiting, Lord.
Renew my strength.

Thank You, faithful God.

# Lord, Don't Let Me Forget Jack!
## Matthew 10:29–31

Of all the students I ever had, Jack was the one most likely to drive me to distraction. He suffered from a limited intelligence, a marked speech defect, the emotional maturity of a preschooler, and other damages from a deprived environment. He lived in poverty with his grandmother and his one surviving parent, as retarded as he.

Jack spent several hours a day in my ninth-grade classroom, even though he had been assigned to me for one class only. I did what I could for him, but it wasn't much. My other, more successful students found his constant presence distracting. The school sent him to speech therapy at a local college and then found a program of vocational rehabilitation that recommended his placement in one of their training institutions. His mother refused to give him up.

"I can't blame her," the counselor admitted.

"Jack had a twin brother who appeared to be more capable. Someone came into the yard one day and shot him. Then Jack's sister was murdered by her estranged husband. Jack is the only child left; his mother won't let him go."

One day Jack labored over a writing assignment and finally turned in a page filled with neatly printed but unintelligible sentences that concluded with this prayer:

Dear God:
     I love you God do you love me.
    God you is me father to help you.
    God came to a hill to see a man.
    God, to feel if there's a place in you
              for me.

I read that over and over.

Is there, God?
Is there a place in You for Jack?
Even the hairs of his head are numbered,
          Lord.

Even the hairs of his head.
Jack has a place in You.
I have a place in You.
You care about both of us.
Let us care about each other.

Cast all your anxieties on him,
for he cares about you.

1 Peter 5:7 RSV

# I Had to "Chasten" Jimmy
## Proverbs 3:11–14

I knew he had been stealing from me; little things kept disappearing, and the evidence always pointed to Jimmy. That day I knew he'd taken my keys from the desk drawer. I asked my husband to go with me to confront Jimmy at home.

His father came to the door. I knew that Jimmy's father sometimes beat him. I suspected that he hoped to keep this son from going to prison like his older brother, and knew no more effective way to deal with him.

Jimmy answered our knock on the door.

"Jimmy," I said firmly, "my keys are missing. Do you know anything about it?"

My husband added quietly, "Jimmy, please

go and get your school jacket and let's see if the keys might be in your pocket."

I turned to the boy's father, who had come up behind him.

"I'd like your promise that you won't whip Jimmy because of this." He promised.

The keys "just happened" to be in Jimmy's jacket pocket. "They must have fallen in there somehow!" he exclaimed.

Then he added, "I just took them to show you how easy it was."

I acknowledged his implied rebuke.

"Well, Jimmy, I guess we've both learned a lesson today."

The boy's father kept his promise. Jimmy never stole from me again.

Ten years later, he looked me up after we had moved to another city, and he brought his wife and baby by to see us. During the visit, he thanked us for caring about him, and told us proudly about his responsible position as manager of the meat market in a large supermarket.

This time, Lord, the discipline turned out
   well.
This time, the student corrected his behavior.
This time, the response was what You
   wanted it to be.

I have not always been so responsive to You,
  Lord.
I have balked at Your rebuke
  and grumbled at Your discipline.
You are my Father;
You have the right and the responsibility to
  correct me.
Thank You for always correcting in love,
  seeking that which is for my own "fullness
  of joy."

A fool spurns his father's discipline, but
  whoever heeds correction shows
            prudence.

Proverbs 15:5

# It Frightens Me to Know What I Can Do to Them
## Psalm 103:13, 14

I remember Raphael. He came into my ninth-grade "special" class, still writing and reading like a first grader. His eyes looked away from mine.

I went to see his mother.

"Raphael went to the first grade, happy and excited, ready to learn just like my other children did. I don't know what happened, but his teacher was harsh with him and he quit learning."

One teacher could do that?

That can't be the whole story, but it frightens me just the same.

Author and teacher Haim Ginott wrote:

I have come to the frightening conclusion that I am the decisive element in the class-

room. It's my personal approach that cre-
ates the climate. It's my daily mood that
makes the weather. As a teacher, I possess
a tremendous power to make a child's life
miserable or joyous. I can be a tool of tor-
ture or an instrument of inspiration. I can
humiliate or humor, hurt or heal. In all
situations, it is my response that decides
whether a crisis will be escalated or de-
escalated, and a child humanized or dehu-
manized.

My students come up to me and I can tell
how important I am to them. The grade I give;
the smile I give or withhold. My bad mood or
headache in the morning may have nothing to
do with them, but they don't know that. They
think they're responsible for all my moods.

Oh, God, help me to be conscious of my
influence, but free me from being so hung up
on it that I can't function as a normal human
being.

Let me be real to my students, Lord.

When I have a headache, remind me to let
them know it's not their fault. When they try
me past endurance, remind me to let them
know that I love them anyway, even when I
can't stand their behavior.

May they see me as human. You above all

others know that "I am dust." You "know my frame." Let me not be embarrassed when my students see my "dust," but let the dust be formed by You into clay in the potter's hand, that my students may see the One who forms me into His own image. May the vessel of my life be filled with Your own love so that my students will remember the love and not the headache.

But this precious treasure—
this light and power that now shine
within us—
is held in a perishable container,
that is, in our weak bodies.
Everyone can see that the glorious power
within
must be from God and is not our own.

2 Corinthians 4:7 TLB

# Can Billy Make It?
## Matthew 18:1–7

Billy was only eight years old, struggling through the third grade. He came to school hungry, he fought with other children, and once he even backed me into a corner by holding a bottle over his head and threatening me with it.

Each morning he came to our resource room before school; our helpful aide gave him a cup of coffee laced with milk and sugar, and usually added a roll or pastry she had brought for him. This experiment with caffeine was designed to control Billy's hyperactivity, but its success may have been due more to the tender loving care than to the caffeine.

The principal told us matter-of-factly,

"He'll end up in jail; nothing you do will change that."

Billy's teacher replied indignantly, "Why are we here if nothing we do makes any difference?"

I'm glad my mother was a teacher who believed in her students. One of her former pupils did go to prison, but he wrote to her and thanked her for believing in him.

She believed in me, too. Once when I worried over an upcoming test (I always worried about grades), she promised, "When you make one hundred on that test, I'll get you that book your music teacher recommended for you."

I continued to fret, "But you won't even help me!" (She helped my brother, and I was jealous, even though she knew I hated to be helped with homework.)

She answered serenely, "I'm sure you'll get the hundred. I'll go ahead and order the book."

She believed in me. I have remembered that tiny incident for more than fifty years.

Billy's chances looked poor. Did we make a difference in what we did with him? Did he have enough people around him believing in him? I wish I knew. He moved away, and I lost track of him.

Children don't always put their potential on
display. Certainly the shepherd boy David
looked less than promising to his own family.
But God passed over David's tall and handsome brothers in order to choose this one
young person whose heart belonged to his
God.

Lord, let me look beneath the surface.
May I not see the discouraging exterior
and believe that there is nothing more to see.
I could not make it unless others believed in
me.
May I also believe in my students.
Show me the gold hidden in the clutter.

∞

Take no account of it if he is handsome
and tall;
. . . The Lord does not see as man sees;
men judge by appearances but the Lord
judges by the heart.
1 Samuel 16:7 NEB

# "Mitchell's Gone to Prison"
## Matthew 25:31–46

I read it in the newspaper. One of my former students had been sent to prison as an accessory to an armed robbery during which a police officer had been injured.

Through a friend active in Prison Fellowship, I contacted Mitchell and asked if I could come to see him. He sent word that he appreciated it, but he didn't want me to see him like that.

Mitchell had a rough childhood. His whole neighborhood suffered from deprivation and violence. When I taught him in the fifth-grade resource room, I saw his struggle with the gaps in his learning.

Mitchell's classroom teacher saw his potential for leadership. She quietly found opportunities for him to demonstrate his strengths. Because of her, he proudly wore a school patrol uniform and assisted other students in crossing the street near the school. In other ways in the classroom, Mitchell became a leader.

Now he was in prison.

I wondered what had happened to that potential.

I began work with a Bible study group in the prison. On each visit, I asked about Mitchell. He finally agreed to see me, and we had a good visit together. He started to attend Bible study and to share his frustrations at the sentence he had received and his intense desire to get out and rejoin his family.

Gradually this young man accepted the opportunities presented to him in the institution. He worked in food service and rose to a supervisory position. What his teachers had seen in him he finally saw in himself. When he came out of prison, he came out to support himself and his family.

Lord, I'm glad that You see my potential.
I'm glad You don't give up on me.
When I disappoint You and land in trouble,

You stick with me and bring me through to
the other side.
No matter what I do, You never stop loving
me.
You never stop reaching out for me.
Thank You for Your persistent love.
Make me willing to reach out my own hand
to those who stumble in the path.

My sacrifice, O God,
is a broken spirit;
a wounded heart, O God,
thou wilt not despise.
Psalm 51:17 NEB

# Trick or Treat!
# Psalm 139:1–6

Sometimes I feel that every day in my class-room is Halloween. My students show me the "face" they think I want to see. Maybe I do the same thing, Lord, with them and with You.

"What you see is what you get"?

Do they give me what I'm looking for?

Michelangelo saw in a piece of marble two figures. From the pink tones in the marble, he carved the figure of a mother; from the white marble came the form of the dead Christ, yet both were carved from the same block because the artist's eye saw the shape of the figures in the cold and lifeless stone.

A deranged man with a hammer attacked the *Pietà* and tried to destroy it. What did he see in that poignant work of art that drove him to violence?

Two visions: One of the artist, who saw in the pink-and-white marble the sensitive form of a grieving mother and a crucified Son. The other, that of a sick mind, threatened in his twisted imagination by the exquisite and the inexplicable, seeking only to destroy that which he could not comprehend.

In Thornton Wilder's play *Our Town*, Emily chose to return to her home and observe the day of her twelfth birthday. Watching the day unfold, she cried, "I can't, I can't go on. It goes so fast! We don't have time to look at each other!"

In our relationships with each other, we are told to "reach for the heart." Behind the front that we put up, each of us has a central core, that unique self that is made in the image of God. We build shells around that vulnerable center in order to protect ourselves from rejection.

When I look at the unformed personalities of my students, I don't always see that vulnerable center. Sometimes I don't even believe that it is there, because of the way they act. I also know that some of them are using mind- and personality-altering substances that make

it even more difficult to reach them where they
live.

Let me take time to look at my students, Lord.
I can't be naive and oblivious to their
problems.
Neither can I assume that what I see is all I
can get.
Let me reach for their hearts.
Let me not attack that which I do not
understand,
but seek for greater perception and insight.

He reveals deep and hidden things;
he knows what lies in darkness,
and light dwells with him.
Daniel 2:22

# I Feel Like a Failure
## Matthew 25:14–30

A college professor once asked a perfectionistic student, "What will you do when you get out into real life where they don't give A's?"

Good grades make us feel successful. That's one reason evaluations threaten teachers. We don't want to be *evaluated* realistically on the basis of what we do well or don't do well. We want to get the "right answers" and get the A and feel successful.

Jesus told a story about three servants: Two got A's and one got an F and was punished. A harsh story. A real life story.

I work with gifted students. So does every teacher, for all students have varying gifts and different ability levels. The landowner in

Jesus' story recognized different levels of potential. He asked simply that each servant be accountable for his investment. The third servant, the one who failed, did not value what he had and feared to risk even that for a master he didn't trust in the first place.

Jesus pointed out the opposite example when He stood to one side and watched people drop their coins in the offering plate in the temple. One widow put in "two very small copper coins" (Luke 21:2), but Jesus said that she gave more than anybody else, because she "out of her poverty put in all she had to live on."

Am I a failure? I look at successful teachers and feel that I, too, have "less than enough." I dread evaluations by strict supervisors, because I know that I will not receive an "outstanding" or "exemplary" rating on everything.

My students don't always succeed. My classroom is not always orderly and the students efficiently occupied when an administrator drops in. My life is not always running smoothly when God looks at me, either.

How does God rate me? Does He have a heavenly evaluation checklist? In Jesus' story, there is a kind of checklist:

1. What did God give me?

2. What have I done with it?

3. Why?

When Jesus told Peter what lay ahead for him, Peter looked at John and asked, "What about him?" Jesus said, in effect, "That's none of your business. Leave John to me" (*see* John 21:18–23).

> Lord, take my eyes off other people
> and what they have or don't have.
> Keep my attention fixed on You,
> that I may love You with my whole heart
> and serve You with all my strength.

Well done, good and faithful servant! . . .
                                        Matthew 25:21

# "The Animals Are My Only Friends"
## Psalm 142:1–7

We sat in a circle, talking about the need to protect our fragile environment. Tommy, a tall, handsome twelve-year-old, had little to say until his turn came in the circle. Tears filled his eyes as he said hesitantly, "I want to take care of the environment because the animals are the only friends I have."

His peers looked at him, astonished that such a bright, good-looking boy, who apparently had "everything going for him" should be that lonely. Once they got over their surprise, they quickly identified with his feelings and encircled him with understanding. It was that kind of group.

Five years later, when I went to a conference at the local high school, a six-foot senior came to the door and asked for me. He knelt by my chair to say with a smile, "Thank you for believing in me. Thank you for helping me find out who I am." He talked about his plans for college, his full life, his exciting studies. Through all of it, I could see his vital circle of friends.

He had to learn to be vulnerable, to reach out and risk his feelings with those who could understand.

I have too often stood apart from those who would have become my friends. I have too often chosen loneliness because I could not admit my need. Jesus said we should become "as little children." He meant the undamaged little child before that beautiful central core experienced rejection or other types of hurt that caused a shell to form around the validated, unique person.

Conformity has become a deadly disease among us. We need to learn to accept our own uniqueness, our validity with God and in so doing celebrate the differences among ourselves.

Thank You, Lord, for those who reached out for me.
Thank You that my long and lonely walk is over.

Make me aware of the loneliness other people
feel.
No matter how successful or unsuccessful
they appear to be,
let me see the real person inside
and be the friend they need me to be.
Thank You for the individuals who have
helped me,
who have become my friends.
Make me aware of the one who stands apart.
Let me reach out my hand and draw that one
into the circle of Your love and mine.

My children,
love must not be a matter of words or
talk;
it must be genuine,
and show itself in action.
1 John 3:18 NEB

# Thanksgiving—All the Time?
## Psalm 34:1–3

On a field trip to Jamestown, Virginia, my students stood at the site of the first little village carved out by settlers who later experienced the "starving time" when most of them died. When I think of Thanksgiving Day and the Pilgrims and Indians of New England with their survival feast, I remember also those unhappy people who starved to death.

Sometimes I think that each student in front of me represents a "new country," with the potential to survive and make it or the threat of perishing in the wilderness. I must help them with their survival skills, as the Indians helped the hapless settlers. When I am seen as an enemy, as some of the early settlers saw the Indians, I can do little to teach survival skills.

When they accept me and I can teach them what they need to know, I give thanks.

The psalmist promised to brag on God at all times, with God's praise always on his lips. His soul boasted in the Lord; he urged the afflicted to pay attention to his boasting and rejoice because of it.

"At all times" covers a lot of ground. We set aside time in November to have a grand splurge of feasting and praise. This makes for a great day! We cook and eat more than we do on any other day of the year. We certainly can't prepare that kind of feast all the time.

I can praise God with my whole heart— sometimes. I can boast about Him— sometimes. Can I really be expected to thank Him and brag on Him *all the time?*

I am no Pollyanna for whom all things forever shine brightly. Clouds descend over my head and the ground slips beneath my feet. The wind blows, the earth shakes, and I become mortally afraid.

In less strenuous times, petty irritations tax my patience and I am totally fed up with trivial nuisances.

In times of great stress or minor mess, can I *honestly* praise God? Boast of Him? Brag on His virtues?

In the midst of nuisances and trials I can
boast of the eternal fact that Jesus loves me;
nothing changes that, not even my own discouragement.

I give You thanks, Father God, that

. . . in all these things we are more than
                    conquerors
        through him who loved us.
For I am convinced that neither death
                    nor life,
        neither angels nor demons,
neither the present nor the future . . .
        nor anything else in all creation,
            will be able to separate us
from the love of God that is in Christ
                Jesus our Lord.
                            Romans 8:37–39

# "This Is a Hard Game"
# John 6:52–68

As we move into the Advent season we enter into the mystery of the Incarnation. How can God become flesh and dwell among us? Like children, we puzzle over what we cannot understand.

Not long ago I found a Chinese checkerboard with wooden pegs. Andrew and I like to play, but he finds the game plan frustrating. Once he said, "This is a hard game, isn't it, Grandmama?"

I love him very much and I try as hard as I can to make the game simple for him. But it *is* a hard game when you're five years old and your grandmother is your "antagonist."

Glyn Evans (in *Daily With the King*) says that "the antagonist relationship is always necessary when the training of minds, souls, or lives is at stake. The classroom teacher is an antagonist. . . . [W]here love enters the picture, the antagonism is greater because love desires the greater growth for the loved one."

Jesus is the ultimate antagonist. The disciples told Jesus that His "game plan" was hard. When He talked about "God made flesh" and the implications of that mystery, even those loyal to Him spoke up. "This is a hard teaching. Who can accept it?"

Aware of their complaints, Jesus continued challenging them with hard teaching. He saw many of His followers drop away discouraged.

"The Word became flesh, and dwelt among us . . ." John said (John 1:14 NAS). The disciples saw His glory, full of grace and truth, but they still did not understand what He tried to tell them.

We continue to live in the mystery of the Incarnation. He dwells among us, full of grace and truth. We receive the reality of His life even when we do not understand the depth of His teaching. He challenges us with "hard sayings."

He is now incarnate in a sense we could never have imagined, for He said, "My Father and I will come to the obedient believer and

make our home with him" (*see* John 14:23).
This is what Leanne Payne (*The Healing Presence*) calls "Incarnational reality, the presence
of God within us."

He walks in our world, crammed as it is with
the pervasive sounds and glittering images of
the season.


Lord Jesus, who came to dwell among us, to
                    dwell in us,
    I get confused by all the noise and
                        rushing about.
    I am swamped by desire.
    The money runs out, the crowd rushes in.
    The work goes on unceasingly.
    In this wonderful Advent season,
    make us overwhelmingly aware of
                Immanuel: God with us.

# If Jesus Came to My School
## Mark 10:13–16

A favorite children's book begins:

> If Jesus came to my house
> and knocked upon the door,
> I'm sure I'd be more happy
> than I've ever been before.

I visited a sixth-grade class and thought of that little rhyme, wondering, *If Jesus came to that school and knocked upon the door, would the children be more happy than they've ever been before?*

In our medium-sized school district there are nearly a thousand classrooms. If Jesus visited six each day, thirty each week, He could spend only one hour per school year in each classroom of one school district in one state in one country!

The Christmas season brings the reminder of Jesus into every schoolroom in one way or another. Even in the exaggerated commercialism there is a loud "knocking" at our door to remind us of the One who stands outside.

If Jesus came into that sixth-grade classroom and asked the teacher, "What do you want Me to do for the children?" I believe she would ask Him, "Please heal their hurts."

She is present with each of her one hundred students for five hours each week, thirty-six weeks in a year. She is patient, kind, accepting, supportive, and loving. She teaches them what she knows and she does it effectively. She can help them learn what they need to know to get along in our world. But she can't heal their hurts.

Satan controls world systems. He wants to steal, kill, and destroy children. But Jesus said that He is greater who is within us ("Incarnational reality") than Satan, who controls the evil that threatens our students.

I want Jesus to visit my classroom. I want Him to stay there all day, every day. The only way He can do that is to take over my own life and love those students through me. During this Advent season, I want to see Christ incarnate in my school.

*Into my heart,*
*into my heart,*
*come into my heart, Lord Jesus.*
*Come in today,*
*come in to stay.*
*Come into my heart, Lord Jesus.*

Then He took them in His arms
and blessed them lovingly, one by one,
laying His hands upon them.

Mark 10:16 WEYMOUTH

# "Teacher, I Brought You a Present"
## Romans 11:33–36

I have a long shopping list for Christmas. If I listed everything I would *like* to be able to give, the list would grow very long indeed. I could add an even longer list of things I would like to have for myself. It would take a very large inheritance to cover both lists.

According to the Bible, we have "inherited the kingdom" of God, for Jesus said that the kingdom of God is within us. He guarantees us all the riches of God Himself!

How can I claim the inheritance that is available to me today?

What is it I *really* need for Christmas?

Is it wisdom?

. . . You teach me wisdom in the inmost place.

Psalm 51:6

Is it patience?

The fruit of the Spirit is . . . patience. . . .
Galatians 5:22

Is it peace?

You will keep in perfect peace him whose
mind is steadfast,
because he trusts in you.
Isaiah 26:3

Is it hope?

. . . My hope comes from him."
Psalm 62:5

Is it strength?

The Lord gives strength to his people. . . .
Psalm 29:11

Is it something else?

My God will meet all your needs
according
to his glorious riches in Christ
Jesus.
Philippians 4:19

Even as the presents I have bought and wrapped are stored up in my house waiting for Christmas Day, so the blessings of God are stored up waiting for me to claim on the day of my need.

How great is your goodness,
which you have stored up for those who fear you,
which you bestow in the sight of men
on those who take refuge in you.
                              Psalm 31:19

Just in the right time, You, Father, will "open your hand, and we will be satisfied with good things" (*see* Psalm 104:28).

Father of all good gifts,
May I receive confidently from Your hand
all the riches of Your mercy stored up for me.

## Christmas Decorations
## Matthew 2:9, 10

I look forward to hanging a Moravian star in our window and adding small twinkling stars to the Christmas tree. Last year Cliff (who is three years old) helped me decorate.

When we brought out the set of ceramic choirboys and placed them on the table, Cliff sang as we added a 1903 *Baptist Hymnal* that belonged to my mother, with its yellowed pages open to Christmas songs. Beside the choirboys, Cliff put a music box, a little church decorated for the season, with an angel coming in and out of the door as the music tinkled "Hark the Herald Angels Sing."

I also look forward to the bright poinsettias in our church. Just outside the large windows at the front of the sanctuary stands a dogwood tree now bright with the red berries of winter. In the spring the tree will be filled with white blooms. Pine and cedars in the forest beyond provide a green background for the dogwood tree.

These symbols of Christmas illumine the darkness of the cold December night. I crave such symbols to light up the darkness in the lives of many of my students. They face the darkness of a world that is cruel to its young. We expose them to pressures they can't understand, much less cope with.

Christmas gives me a welcome interlude. I can see my work more objectively when I can get away from it for a few days. I can breathe deeply of Christmas spices and fresh bread. I can revel in the decorative symbols and almost convince myself that peace reigns on earth and goodwill is present in the lives of all my students.

My mother reminded us often that "Merry Christmas is for children; a joyous Christmas is for believers." She never entered into the "happiness" of Christmas, for the greatest tragedy of her life, the death of my father, came early in December, and each year thereafter brought fresh reminders of her grief. But she experienced the *joy* of Christmas, all year round.

I will take down the decorations before I return to school after the holidays, but the beauty and joy they gave to me will stay with me for the rest of the year.

Father, thank You.
Thank You for the symbols of the season.
Thank You for the children who sing.
Thank You for the gifts given in lovingkindness.
Thank You that the Christ Child is never lost even in the confusion of this Christmas season.

. . . You are to give him the name Jesus, because he will save his people from their sins.

Matthew 1:21

## Return to Your Rest
## Psalm 116:7–9

I need You today, Lord. I am tired and dispirited. The holidays are too much with me, with the endless trivia, the consumption mentality, unceasing "busyness," and the never-ending clamor of television.

How can I be so petty? This is my vacation! I have what I craved just two weeks ago, when I counted the days before Christmas holidays.

I remember that the Bible often mentions *rest*. I don't think it's talking about sleeping late.

This is what the Lord says:
Stand at the crossroads and look;
ask for the ancient paths,
ask where the good way is,

and walk in it,
and you will find rest for your souls. . . .
Jeremiah 6:16

Take my yoke upon you and learn from
me . . .
and you will find rest for your souls.
Matthew 11:29

I find warnings, too:

. . . Their hearts are always going astray,
and they have not known my ways . . .
they shall never enter my rest.
Hebrews 3:10, 11

I apparently "stand at a crossroads" and yearn for a kind of rest that is beyond physical relief. I watch my friend Delores going through difficulties and physical strain beyond my comprehension, as she literally supports the weight of her sixteen-year-old daughter who struggles to overcome the effects of a brain tumor. Yet Dee finds rest in the midst of physical exhaustion, because she fully accepts what You give to her in each moment of her day. She has what is described as a "cheerful and buoyant spirit, and peace in doing Thy will" (John Baillie, *Diary of Private Prayer*).

She walks in "the ancient paths, . . . where the good way is." This path You placed before Abraham when You promised the impossible and asked Your servant to believe You. I must believe You for my path, too.

You meet me exactly where I am today. You know the circumstances of my life. You only ask that I let You control me in the midst of those circumstances, and feel the weight of the responsibility roll off my shoulders and onto the only One capable of carrying me through it all.


*I receive Your rest, Father.*
*I receive that deep relief that comes from knowing*
  *that You are in charge, and that*
  *"all things shall be well,*
  *and all manner of things shall be well,*
  *and you shall see it in truth,*
  *in the fulness of joy."*

Juliana of Norwich

. . . His resting place will be glorious.
Isaiah 11:10 NAS

# Starting Over
## Psalm 40:3; 98:1

I would like to go back to school after the holidays with a "new song in my mouth," even "praise to our God." Where will this "new song" come from? How can I "sing it to the Lord"?

We looked forward to the long break at Christmas. First semester moved quickly. Once we got settled in to our classes, with occasional days off, the seasons rolled past, through Halloween, Thanksgiving, and the music and madness of Christmas. Seasonal decorations went up and came down with astonishing speed.

Now it's winter, and the holidays are behind us. My students will be looking back, too. The excitement has died away; we are back to "business as usual."

We look ahead to a long stretch before spring break. The few days off at that time seem far away.

I liked being at home for the holidays. I enjoyed the freedom of flexible time with family and friends.

At this point in the "winter of my life," where does a new song come from?

Not from my circumstances. They change too much.

Not from my feelings. If I depended on feelings, my moods would resemble a weather vane, swinging in all directions.

Not from other people. They are bogged down in their own concerns.

This new song can come only from my God.

When I wait patiently for Him, He turns to me and hears my cry for help. He has set my feet on a rock, giving me a firm place to stand. That rock is the confidence that He loves me. He accepts me exactly as I am. He knows how I feel today. He never changes, no matter how much I may change, or how much the world around me may change.

Jeremiah was called the "weeping prophet" because of his cries to God over the pitiable conditions of the people he loved. Yet his lamentations included a song of praise to God in the midst of difficult circumstances.

> . . . his compassions never fail.
> They are new every morning;
> great is your faithfulness.
>                    Lamentations 3:22, 23

Faithful God,
  As I return to my responsibilities
  May I take with me in my heart
  and in my mouth
  a new song to sing.
  A song of Your faithfulness to me,
  Your mercies, which are new every
                    morning.

# "What Can I Do Now?"
# Psalm 139:13–16; Matthew 20:26

When our first grandchild was born, we were there to greet his entrance into the world.

"Andrew, this is Granddaddy! This is Grandmama!"

From the time his eyes were barely open, he saw that we accepted him, loved him, and made him a part of our lives.

Now that he is five, when Andrew comes to our house he wants only two things: to be with one or both of us and to help us to do whatever it is we're doing. At the end of one task, he'll say eagerly, "What can I do now?"

I look at him and wonder, *Am I like that little child?* You, Father, were there when I was born. You surrounded me with Your love. You made me a part of all that You were doing. You

invited me to help You in Your work. To Andrew, it doesn't matter much what we're doing as long as we're doing it together.

Do I want to be with You that much?

Do I run as eagerly to help You as Andrew
runs to help me?

In *The Practice of the Presence of God*, Brother
Lawrence wrote:

> The time of business does not with me dif-
> fer from the time of prayer, and in the
> noise and clatter of my kitchen, while sev-
> eral persons are at the same time calling for
> different things, I possess God in as great
> tranquillity as if I were upon my knees at
> the blessed sacrament.

Brother Lawrence delighted in "taking up a
straw from the ground for the love of God."

In my work I meet people who remind me
of Brother Lawrence. I look forward to seeing
"Preacher Bryant" walking around the hall-
ways in our high school. The first time I saw
him, he sat at a desk near the door, waiting for
a meeting to end so that he could lock up the
building. In front of him he had a worn Bible,
nearly falling apart. After any conversation
with him, I always come away sensing the
presence of God.

I see that same presence in the smile on Ola Mae's face as she keeps the windows at the entrance of our middle school sparkling clean. Both of these special people take delight in their work because they do it for the love of God.

My students are my assignment for today. Each of them is a "straw" I can pick up for the love of God.

∽

I no longer call you servants,
because a servant does not know his
master's business.
Instead, I have called you friends,
for everything that I learned from
my Father
I have made known to you.
You did not choose me,
but I chose you and appointed you
to go and bear fruit—
fruit that will last.

John 15:15, 16

# Cactus Thorns and Blooms
## Isaiah 35:1–4

Walking around my neighborhood, I watch a sturdy cactus plant, green and thriving. Yesterday I saw again the sharp, forbidding thorns, but in the center of the plant had grown large purple pods that indicate the ultimate arrival of beautiful cactus flowers.

I thought of the students I have known who held me off with their hostile, sharp "thorns" of a rebellious attitude. I drew back from them, afraid of those thorns. Sometimes I even got hurt by their getting "under my skin."

These have not been my favorite students. They are the ones I'd rather have assigned to another class. But when I saw that cactus plant, I remembered the surprises I have had with some of these prickly students whose lives have now blossomed with fragrant, exotic, lavish blooms.

Cactus plants survive on a minimum of moisture. They have to draw deeply from dry soil to maintain enough liquid for life. Their enemies would devour them readily if they did not produce discouraging thorns.

I discovered that survival strength is a characteristic of people with significant gifts and provides the stubborn persistence that protects those gifts in destructive environments. That very strength may reveal itself in prickly behavior. Vulnerable children put up defenses to protect themselves against rejection and repeated hurt. If I also am struggling to survive within my own insecurities and vulnerabilities, then "thorn meets thorn" and we hurt each other.

I'm glad that God my Father does not see only the surface thorns. When the prodigal son decided to go home, his father ran to meet him, gathered him close, and made him welcome. He put aside the memory of the rebellious, reckless spirit that had separated them (Luke 15:11–24).

Amy Carmichael said, "Never mind my feelings: the one thing that matters is not to stay away from you, Lord, because of them."

Lord, when my thorns surface
and my flowers are slow to bloom,
send my roots deeper into the soil of Your
love
that I may draw the water of life into my
being
and experience that spring of water
welling up to eternal life.

But whoever drinks the water I give him
will never thirst.
Indeed, the water I give him
will become in him a spring of water
welling up to eternal life.

John 4:14

# "It Hurts!"
# Hebrews 4:15, 16

Little Libby is not quite two years old. She had a booster shot the day before she came to visit us, and her leg was very sore from the shot. When her daddy called to check on her, she held the telephone and whimpered, "It hurts."

Her daddy understood. He did not yell at her for not "speaking up." He did not ridicule her complaint, even though he knew that the pain was temporary and not terribly serious. All that mattered to her and to her daddy was that "it hurts right now."

Her parents have helped Libby acquire an extensive vocabulary. She happily sings and chatters freely and clearly. On this day, she did neither. She only felt like saying to her daddy, "It hurts."

Sometimes I can talk to God freely and praise Him with a "loud voice." Many times I can only manage to whisper to Him, "It hurts." I know He understands. He does not rebuke me for complaining nor insist that I speak up clearly. He sees my particular pain in the right perspective, but He also feels that pain with me and understands the present anguish.

A friend once said to me, "I tried to pray, but all I could do was cry; I thought later that those tears may have been the first completely honest prayer of my life."

I am glad that we have in Jesus a High Priest who is able to sympathize with our weaknesses because He felt all the pain and temptation we feel. He has "been there." Jesus Himself "learned [the meaning of] obedience from the things which He suffered" (Hebrews 5:8 NAS).

On the day twelve-year-old Lee's mother died, Lee was attending a summer workshop in our district. During the months that followed, he clung to his teacher. His emotional dependency wore her out sometimes, but she knew that she had to be there for him.

At times like that, she realizes that being a teacher is more than rules and regulations, textbooks and examinations. Being a teacher means standing in the gap to meet the needs of her students.

Lord, help me to understand
how my students feel when they hurt.
May they see that I know how they feel
when all they can say inside is, "It hurts."
Through me, show them the Father
who completely understands,
and makes it possible for us to call Him
"Abba."

"By His Spirit, we can call Him,
'Abba [daddy], Father'."
*See* Romans 8:15

# "One of the Parents Told Me Off Today"
## 1 Peter 2:18–23

I can't believe a parent would talk to me that way! I tried as hard as I could to help that student, but I got blamed for everything *she* failed to do!

When I went into the teachers' lounge for lunch, I could not hold back the tears. When the other teachers asked me what was wrong, I spilled out my frustrations and overwhelming sense of failure.

As they jumped to my defense, I knew that I was surrounded by caring, accepting, understanding people. They were great! They've been there. They know how I feel. They know how unfair parents can be when their children have problems the parents themselves don't know how to cope with.

I need help, too, Lord. I need my friends. I need understanding. I need acceptance. I need to be appreciated.

Most of all, I need to feel *valid*. When I face criticism that I consider unjust, the life drains out of my teaching. That makes me feel sad, but it does help me to empathize with students who lose their "bubble" in an unaccepting, inflexible environment.

I can refuse to be stifled on a permanent basis. You will open doors for me in Your own time.

Most of all, I thank You that YOU understand. I thank You that You alone know my heart and You accept me "warts and all."

You suffered abuse beyond any that I can even imagine.

You suffered the misunderstanding of the people in Your hometown, who thought they knew You better than anybody else did. You even suffered the misunderstanding of Your own family, who openly wondered if You were "beside Yourself," or out of Your mind.

Thank You for what teachers give to one another. I am glad that there are those who believe in me.

Let me remember that "Thou art not the more holy, if thou art praised, nor the more worthless, if thou art found fault with. What thou art, thou art. . . . Man looks on the deeds, but God weighs the intentions" (Thomas à Kempis in *The Imitation of Christ*).

Finally, all of you,
live in harmony with one another;
be sympathetic, love as brothers,
be compassionate and humble.
Do not repay evil with evil, or insult with insult,
but with blessing,
because to this you were called
so that you may inherit a blessing.

1 Peter 3:8, 9

## "How's Your Heart?"
## Psalm 57:7–11

I like Valentine's Day. Many of the staff and students get valentines with red roses and balloons. Even when the gestures are meant as a joke, the "heart" comes through. We can give and receive the genuine affection we feel for each other. Maybe it is mostly sentimental and superficial, but it's fun!

On the other hand, I sometimes hear people say sarcastically, "You're all heart," meaning anything but that.

What does the Bible say about my "heart condition"?

> . . . out of the overflow of the heart the
> mouth speaks.
>
> Matthew 12:34

. . . Give me an undivided heart. . . .
Psalm 86:11


I will give them an undivided heart
and put a new spirit in them;
I will remove from them
their heart of stone
and give them a heart of flesh.
Ezekiel 11:19


This obviously does not mean bypass sur-
gery or heart transplants. The meaning of *heart*
goes much deeper in Scripture (and also in
valentines!).

This "heart of mine" controls my desires. It
turns toward the things I deeply cherish. It
centers on one primary object, that which I
love more than anything else in the world.

When I pray, "Search me, and know my
heart," I am really praying, "Examine my priorities." Find out what I care about. After all,
my students "don't care what I know, they
want to know that I care."

Too often I love me, and I use my students
to build up my own self-image as a successful
teacher. Their indifference, or inadequacy, or
failure somehow reflects on me, their teacher,
and I resent it.

To truly "give my heart" is to love something or someone *as it is*, not as I wish it were. This kind of acceptance is difficult for me to give, even to God, because I often would like Him to be different, more tailored to what I hope He will do for me.

Madame Guyon said, "To love Him is to love everything about Him, even that which we do not understand."

God my Father,
  On this special day, I want to love You as
    You are.
  I give to You my heart in its real condition.
  I ask You for a new heart, undivided,
  Full of the love You have for me,
  Spilling over into the hearts of my students.

  Search me, O God, and know my
        heart. . . .
                    Psalm 139:23

# God Rebukes; Satan Accuses
## Psalm 6:1–4

God rebukes and reproves me in order to discipline me.
>   Satan denounces and taunts me in order to destroy me.

God rebukes me because He loves me.
>   Satan accuses me because he hates me.

God "shapes up" one in whom He delights.
>   Satan tears down one whom he despises.

God seeks to purify the gold He sees in me.
>   Satan seeks to bury the good he sees in me.

God gives reassurance that I belong to Him.
>   Satan tells me I belong to no one, ever.

God removes the clutter from my life.
>   Satan fills my life with garbage.

God breaks the chains that hold me in captivity.

Satan locks the chains and throws away the
    key.
God reassures me.
    Satan frightens me.
God clarifies.
    Satan confuses.
God gives me hope.
    Satan causes me to despair.
God tells me how valuable I am.
    Satan convinces me I'm worthless.
God's rebuke is loving and tender.
    Satan's accusations are harsh and bitter.
God encourages me when I am "down."
    Satan discourages me when I am "up."
God gives me strength to endure.
    Satan makes me want to give up.
When I rebuke my students, whose side am I
    on?
    Do I build up or tear down?
    Do I encourage or discourage?
    Do I love them or despise them?
    Do I give them strength or take it away?


Lord, You know that I am not always clear
            about my motives.
    Sometimes I can't tell whether it's the
            behavior
        or the person I dislike.
    I take delight in "telling them off"

when they upset me and make me look bad.
I don't want to hurt them.
I want them to understand that they have to
behave.
They have to conform to a reasonable
standard
if any learning is to take place.
Help me to give to them what I count on Your
giving to me.

My Son . . . do not lose heart when he
rebukes you,
because the Lord disciplines those he
loves. . . .
Hebrews 12:5, 6

# That Which Cannot Be Shaken
## Hebrews 12:26–28

Leaving the city of Chicago recently, I passed an old public school building and saw, carved into the stone facade above the entrance at one end of the school, the inscription "Girls' Entrance." I assumed that I could have found at the other end of the building a similar doorway marked "Boys' Entrance."

Whoever chiseled those directives into the very stones of the building believed that the school's policy of separate sex entrances would never change.

How quickly the mores of our society made those labels obsolete!

What today do we assume "will always be this way," when in fact a change will come, and very quickly?

Using the Bible as a "teacher's manual," I
discover that some things cannot be shaken
out of education.

We will always need
     a teacher to teach,
     a student to respond,
     and content that makes sense of our
        world.
   These "unshakens" will provide a way
     to understand that I am a worthwhile
        human being,
     to learn how to get along with other
        people,
     to laugh,
     and to feel successful.


Some things have been shaken
and will be shaken again and again,
and some will disappear entirely, unlamented:
        this building style,
        that textbook,
        this teaching method.
But always, there must be careful guidance,
       strengthening encouragement,
    and practical assistance with the task.


Lord, You know how quickly things change.
   You see the bewildering assault of
        information.

You are not overwhelmed, as we are, by our
technology.

Give to me a steady heart.
Let me not be overcome by the pressures of
the age.
Keep my eyes fixed on that which cannot be
shaken,
because it rests on the solid foundation
of the Lord our God.

And He shall be the stability of your
times,
A wealth of salvation, wisdom, and
knowledge. . . .

Isaiah 33:6 NAS

# Take Courage
## 2 Thessalonians 2:16, 17

Several years ago, my students and I went to a local park for an end-of-the-year outing. They got together a softball game and persuaded me to come up to bat.

I swatted at a few balls and managed to connect with one well enough to head for first base. They threw faster than I could run and I was "out at first."

As I trudged off the playing field, a seventh grader ran up to give me a hug. "That's all right, Mrs. Ward. We can't all be good at everything!"

She comforted me again when we went on a field trip to Washington. The students did not cooperate as well as they should have, and I became anxious and upset. After I yelled at them in frustration, they silently lined up to get on the bus. When she came up beside me, Wyn stopped and said with a bright smile, "Do you need a hug?"

Relieved, I quickly responded, "I can't think of anything I need more!" My bad mood evaporated with her reassurance.

Recently one of the women in our Bible study group said in frustration, "What I need is a Dick-and-Jane Bible!"

She needed plain language, something she could understand and identify with her own life. The next week, a friend in the group brought her a "plain English" Bible, and she has enjoyed it tremendously. The language she could relate to gave her courage to study the Bible.

The prophet Ezra became terribly discouraged over the sinful condition of the people of God. As he wept and prayed, the people around him repented, and they said to him, "there is still hope for Israel. . . . We will support you, so take courage and do it."

Jesus told His disciples, "Take courage." Those around us offer us courage. We can *take courage*, and go on.

Lord, my heart often faints within me.
I grow anxious and troubled,

dismayed about what is pressing in, all
around,
and fearful about what may yet come into my
life.
Show me how to hope in God,
who daily bears my burdens
and strengthens my heart with courage.

And . . . Jonathan went to David
. . . and helped him find strength in God.
1 Samuel 23:16

Wait for the Lord;
Be strong, and let your heart take
courage. . . .
Psalm 27:14 NAS

# Sparrows
## Psalm 84:3; Matthew 10:29–31

Not one sparrow falls without my heavenly
Father.
But the sparrow *does fall*,
and God is with the sparrow
as it falls.

Even so,

He enters into our falling,
into our griefs,
into our sins,
into our foolish faltering,
and He is there.

I see so many "sparrows" in my classes.
They look hurt and troubled; I don't know

what to do about it. I know that I am not God;
I can't fix the world and everything in it. I
wonder why God, who *is* God, doesn't fix the
world so that sparrows would not fall from the
nest, and my students would not be hurt by all
the fallenness around them.

Francis Schaeffer reminded us that we live in
a fallen world and God shares with us the fallenness. He did not cause us to fall, but He
shares with us the hurt and heals the brokenness.

I sometimes think that God stands beside
the fallen sparrow, unmoved and helpless. But
He does not stand there unmoved, and I cannot either. It matters to Him, the falling.


Lord,
       when the way is dark before me,
         and I cannot see my way,
       give me grace to seek your light.
      When I know that I am falling,
      let me feel the everlasting arms
         that are beneath me,
      the solid rock beneath my feet.
      When I cannot see the whole,
     give me grace to take the one step
      that opens plain before my eyes.

*I falter where I firmly trod,*
*and falling with my weight of cares*
*upon the great world's altar-stairs,*
*that slope through darkness up to God,*
*I stretch lame hands of faith, and grope. . . .*

From "In Memoriam"
by Alfred, Lord Tennyson

. . . don't be afraid; you are worth more
than many sparrows.

Matthew 10:31

## Tests and Measurements
## Psalm 26:2, 3; Matthew 25:31–45

I'm sitting here facing my lesson plans for the next study unit. I know that I must set specific goals, with "behavioral outcomes" that can be measured. My students must learn that which tests measure. I have to mark their progress in that learning and indicate their success or failure on printed reports that go to parents.

Everything I do must "pay off" in such measurable ways. I myself am evaluated on how well I can present a lesson that includes all the elements thought to be essential to successful teaching.

I wish I could take a look at Your "lesson plan" for me, Lord. What are Your "goals" for me today?

I confess that I don't usually know what Your "objective" is. I muddle through my life, hoping to succeed in reaching Your goals, but I don't get many "report cards" from the heavenly desk.

My students don't always know what I'm trying to do, either. I want them to establish their own goals, and I hope that those goals are reasonably in line with my own objectives for their learning. Their goals and mine should relate to the textbooks we have adopted as guides.

I do see Your standard in Your textbook, the Bible, and I recognize that Your measurement of success is not the same as mine. I always want to know that I have succeeded. I don't want anybody to see me as a failure. I especially don't want to see myself as a failure. How do You see me, Lord?

You rank faithfulness and obedience as essential goals. Can these be measured?

You do test us. You certainly do. You test our obedience. I have often failed that test. When I decide to have my own way, I fail the test of obedience. I sometimes give up when the going gets rough and fail the test of faithfulness.

I read recently of a teacher who retired after

forty-five years of service. One of his friends said that the highest compliment he could give him was to congratulate him on showing up! After forty-five years of teaching, that is really an accomplishment, to show up and keep at it.

Sometimes it's all I can do to "show up." Drag out of bed and get there to face all that is waiting for me. You know that my students often feel the same way.

Lord,
>      Thank You that You give us credit
>           for victory
>      even when the most we can do
>           some days is just show up.

Well done, good and faithful servant! . . .
                                    Matthew 25:21

# How Do You Define Waste?
## John 6:12, 13; 12:1–8

Sometimes it appears that You're not very efficient in the allocation of human resources, Lord. When You fed five thousand people, You had the disciples gather up all the broken pieces of bread and fish so that none would be wasted. Yet when Mary broke a flask of expensive ointment over Your head, You applauded her over the protests of Your disciples, who naturally thought about how much the sale of such perfume would bring to the "purse for the poor."

To *waste* is to "spend or be spent uselessly."

The concept of waste ties in to our value system. Broken food fragments can feed people, and people are valuable. The complaining disciples called Mary's actions "wasteful" because they did not value You as much as Mary did.

In this morning's newspaper I read that the president of a thriving Bible college and seminary, after twenty-two years of successful leadership, resigned his position in order to take care of his ailing wife, who suffers from a form of dementia. They have been faithful servants of Yours during forty-five years of marriage. He's healthy and useful. What sense does it make for him to assume the role of servant to a sick wife?

He explained it simply: "When my wife became ill, I said immediately that when the time came that she would need me full-time, she would have me. That time has come." He added, "I love her."

No one can call wasted that which is lavished on a deeply cherished and valuable person.

I see enormous waste in the classroom. I see students with bright minds throwing their lives away on drugs that damage their brains. I see others struggling with great limitations, trying to learn.

Would it not be more "efficient" in Your grand plan to give the great potential to those who would not waste it? Are not the conscientious students more deserving of great gifts?

Could I then call useless those students who blindly destroy their lives? You call no man useless. You hold each accountable for what he does with what he has.

A fourteenth-century mystic wrote, "It is not what you are nor what you have been that God sees with his all-merciful eyes, but what you desire to be" (*The Cloud of Unknowing*).

For my thoughts are not your thoughts,
neither are your ways my ways . . .
As the heavens are higher than the earth,
so are my ways higher than your ways
and my thoughts than your thoughts.
Isaiah 55:8, 9

## Fly to the Mountain!
## Psalm 11:1; Psalm 30

After the long months of winter, I can hardly wait for spring break. I agree with my friend Betty, who wrote from the mountains of north Georgia:

"What a difference a mountain can make
in my world!
. . . everything happy
. . . everything good
. . . everything beautiful."

We all need our "mountains of refuge," those places of comfort and healing to which we can fly when life gets too much to stand.

When the crush of work catches us and pushes us down, the next thing we know, we

are groveling in the dust. We desperately need
a change of perspective.

The mountain of God's truth gives us this
"scenic overlook."

> The eternal God is your refuge,
> and underneath
> are the everlasting arms. . . .
> Deuteronomy 33:27

> God is our refuge and strength,
> an ever-present help in trouble.
> Psalm 46:1

> I lift up my eyes to the hills—
> where does my help come from?
> My help comes from the Lord,
> The Maker of heaven and earth.
> Psalm 121:1

> Blessed be the Lord, who daily bears our
> burden. The God who
> . . . has commanded your strength. . . .
> Psalm 68:19, 28 NAS

In *Edges of His Ways*, Amy Carmichael wrote:

> *But when from mountain top,*
>     *My Lord, I look with Thee,*
> *My cares and burdens drop*
>     *Like pebbles in the sea.*
> *The air is clear,*
>     *I fear no fear,*
>     *In this far view*
>     *All things are new.*

Lord
  You know the depths of the valley.
  You know the crush of duties and delights.
  You know that I need a change of
      perspective.
  Thank You for spring holidays.
  Let this become a time for me to see as You
      see.
  Let me catch a glimpse of the long view,
  the beauty of Your plan,
  the perfection of Your purpose for my life.
  And when I return to my students,
  may my eyes be clearer and my heart at
      peace.

. . . Come, let us go up to the mountain
of the Lord. . . . He will teach us his ways,
  so that we may walk in his paths. . . .

Micah 4:2

# Cracked Foundations
## Psalm 11:3–7

When Larry's company transferred him to another city, he and Jean put their house on the market. The appraisers discovered that the beautiful home rested on a foundation that had cracked beyond repair. The young couple faced a drastic loss in the value of their property.

When Hurricane Hugo struck South Carolina, the houses built on landfill or sand toppled into the ocean. The devastation of the storm revealed the strength of the foundations.

Many of my students appear to be fine on the surface of their lives until I discover that their foundations are cracked beyond repair. The essential needs of acceptance, belonging,

and self-esteem have gone unmet in their
lives.

Can I help rebuild their lives on a better
foundation?

My favorite house in our community is large
and well-constructed, but it stood empty for
several years, the once-immaculate yard lit-
tered with debris, and the cluttered interior of
the house showing through uncurtained windows. The basically sound property looked
unkempt and unloved.

Some of my students look like that. Their
lives have had a good foundation, but they are
cluttered with the "garbage" of carelessness
and neglect. What can I do?

I was relieved when someone bought that
empty house, cleaned up the debris, turned
on the lights, moved in, and began to cherish
the property. I wish I could encourage my students to clean up the debris in their lives, turn
on the lights, and cherish what they have.

Lord,
    It bothered me to see an attractive house
            deteriorating.
    It bothers me much more to see young lives
            deteriorating.
        I worry about cracking foundations

in the families of our community.
I worry about my own children and
grandchildren.
Show me what I can do to "shore up the
foundations"
for my students and for my family,
to help them clean out the junk
and live strong and sure in a world
that has been made dependable for them.

When the foundations are being
destroyed, what can the
righteous do?
Psalm 11:3

# Looking On, With Love
## Mark 10:17–22

Recently I said smugly to my son, "Cliff loves his grandmama." Charles answered thoughtfully, "I've noticed that. He does love you. It's because you pay attention to him."

I do pay attention to Cliff. I listen to him (it's not hard) and I really *see* him. (That's not hard, either—he's beautiful!) I get right into what he's doing, playing with small trucks on the carpet, making a "circus ring" out of blocks, or pretending that we're both riding in a fire truck (he's the driver).

I like watching his three-year-old mind come alive and learn. In education courses, I've learned some things about the brain and its electrical impulses. Attention literally "sparks" the brain into action, as a "current" flows between two minds.

I can see this in my students, and I am reminded of them when I read about Jesus and the rich young ruler. Jesus paid full attention to the question this young man asked and then gave him the answer he probably expected: "Keep the commandments."

He watched as the man's face fell. The young seeker had hoped for more. All of his careful law-keeping had not filled the vacuum in his life. Jesus seized this "teachable moment" and got his full attention: "If you really want to find what you're looking for, sell all you have and give it to the poor [or, get rid of whatever is in your way] and come with me as my disciple. *Then* you'll find what you're looking for." Even when the young man turned away from such a high price, Jesus gazed full at him, regretting the decision, loving him in his hunger and emptiness.

My students don't always "come through" for me. Can I look at them lovingly even when they disappoint me? Even when I know they make bad decisions? Can I give my attention only to those who please me, thinking it a waste of time to pay attention to those who don't seem to "give a rip"?

How can I find time for all this attention-giving?

I have papers to grade, lessons to prepare. I don't have time for all I must do. Or do I?

Jesus had three public years. He gave His full attention to individuals He met. I've had forty "public years" already. How much time do I need to love someone? To "gaze on him lovingly, with my full attention"?

Lord,
   Teach me to look on each one and love him.

Dear children,
let us not love with words or tongue
but with actions and in truth.
                    1 John 3:18

# I'd Like a Clean Cup, Please
## Matthew 15:10–20

The coffee drinkers in the school keep individual cups in the teachers' lounge. Often when I stop by, someone will offer me a cup of coffee and will wash the cup before giving it to me. They know that I'd like a clean cup.

The other day I heard myself say something that I instantly regretted. To my chagrin, I realized that when I snap at somebody, that "snappishness" is in my heart before it can come out of my mouth. As a reasonably mature adult, I can usually "clamp a lid on my mouth." I can "strain out" the ugliness before it "pours into the cup."

What I *really* want is to get the pitcher clean so that I won't need the strainer! If no anger or ugliness is inside, none can come out.

Early in my teaching career, I had a supervisor whom I mistakenly considered a threat to "my program" because I thought his goals differed from mine. I shared my frustration at the dinner table one night.

The very next day, this man visited my daughter's high school English class. When he was introduced, she said impulsively, "Oh, you're the one my mother was telling me about! Why do you want to destroy her program?"

When she told me about it, I was appalled. Fearing for my job, I hurried to the supervisor to apologize, but he laughed at my concern, adding thoughtfully, "It didn't bother me for her to say that. It did upset me to think that one of my teachers could consider me a threat." What was in my heart (insecurity) showed up in my mouth (misunderstanding). What was in his heart (acceptance) showed up in his speech (caring).

Fill a cup to the brim with sweet water,
    and only sweet water can spill out.
Fill a mind with sweetness,
    and only sweetness can spill out.
Crush a rose petal,
    and a sweet fragrance will be released.

Only God can "cleanse my cup"
    and "fill my petals" with a sweet
                        perfume.

Lord,
            I want to *feel* kind and gentle,
    all the way to the brim of my personality,
        so that what comes out of my mouth
                will be kind and gentle.
            You know the aggravations.
    You know my insecurities and frustrations.
                You know my heart.
            Cleanse my "cup" for me.

∽

Cleanse me with hyssop, and I will be
clean; wash me, and I will be whiter
                than snow.
                            Psalm 51:7

# Potpourri and Perfume
## John 12:1–3

If I were led blindfolded into a school, I would instantly recognize that traditional aroma, which is probably a mixture of young wiggly bodies, cleaning products, years of chalkdust, and teacher fatigue.

Our schools get periodic visits from a drug-detection team that includes a trained dog who can quickly sniff out the presence of drugs in a student's locker. The student may sit in front of me with drugs in his pocket, and I'll never detect it, but with its keen sense of smell the animal picks up the traces of a forbidden substance.

In *Edges of His Ways*, Amy Carmichael says:

> *Fragrance is like light.*
> *It cannot be hidden.*

*It is like love, intangible, invisible*
*but always at once recognized.*
*Its opposite is just as impossible to hide,*
*and though it is neither to be touched,*
*nor heard, nor seen,*
*we know that it is there.*
*. . . It is what we are that tells.*

It is in the "crunch" that the odor is released. When I feel the crunch, my personality sends off that which is inside me. If the bottle is filled with perfume, crushing the vial produces an incredibly sweet fragrance. If the bottle is filled with bitterness, the odor will be bitter and unpleasant.

What smell is released from the crunch of my circumstances? Do my students walk into a room filled with the fragrance of love or with the bitterness of rejection?

I think I'd better give my classroom a "nose test"!

Lord,
   My students may not hear me sometimes,
   they may not see what I want them to see,
but I know that their sense of "smell" is keen.
Check me out, Lord.
      I don't really want to be "broken"

I don't enjoy the crunch of circumstances.
But in the crunch and breaking open
of that which is deep inside myself,
may the odor that pours forth
be one of sweetness and lovingkindness.

*Let the touch of Thy blessed feet*
*turn my poor offering*
*into something sweet to Thee and to others.*
                    Amy Carmichael

. . . the house was filled with the
fragrance of the perfume.
                    John 12:3

# What's So Funny?
# Genesis 17:17; 18:10–15;
# Psalm 126

We live in a ridiculous world. We park on driveways and drive on parkways, pronounce *ough* many different ways, and call children "slow" when they can't figure it all out!

I take myself far too seriously. I always have. But I enjoy reading about Abraham's falling on his face laughing at what God had told him. "Me? Have a son when my wife and I are too old even to think about it?" Sarah laughed, too, but the last laugh was Yours, Lord, because one year later that old couple had their son Isaac.

Even the question You asked was funny: "Is anything too hard for God?" As J. B. Phillips says, that kind of God is obviously too small.

You asked Job, "You can't even challenge a crocodile! What makes you think you can stand against me?" (*see* Job 41).

Did Jesus laugh? Of course He did! For thirty years He watched the growing up of the children playing around the carpenter shop in Nazareth. No one could become the Master Teacher without learning to laugh a lot. He ridiculed those who "strained out gnats and swallowed camels." (They must have been educators!)

In using a new teacher evaluation form, I discovered that the weakest point in the demonstration was usually "shows a sense of humor." Even that struck me as ridiculous. How can a new teacher, striving earnestly to get it all right, be funny in front of an official evaluator poised to write down everything?

Isn't it funny that we have to research and justify laughter as somehow "useful" in education? The Bible got way ahead of us on that.

". . . The joy of the Lord is your strength" (Nehemiah 8:10). Nehemiah battled stern critics of his own, but kept his joy.

"A cheerful heart is good medicine . . ." (Proverbs 17:22).

". . . Wisdom brightens a man's face and changes its hard appearance" (Ecclesiastes 8:1). Does my "wisdom" brighten my face?

I can't be filled with joy and not laugh easily, for that kind of laughter comes from a freed-up heart.

A serious symptom of emotional illness is the inability to laugh. A grave indication of spiritual sickness also is the inability to laugh, especially at myself.

Lord,
    forgive my spells of dreadful seriousness.
    Give me a merry and joyful heart
    because my inward self sees what You see
        and rejoices.

I have told you this so that my joy may be in you and that your joy may be complete.

John 15:11

## Confrontation
## Genesis 2:18; Ecclesiastes 4:10;
## Psalm 142:4

I first saw him with his grandmother, who was attending a teachers' conference. He sat over in a corner in the library where the group met. He appeared to be so "out of it" that I assumed he was mentally retarded.

Later I met the exceptionally bright Ronnie when he came into the gifted program in the fourth grade. The other students tried to include him in their activities, but he preferred to keep his distance. He even crawled under the furniture or wandered around the room. To get his attention, the group called out, "Earth to Ronnie, earth to Ronnie, come in, Ronnie!" and he'd laugh pleasantly and join them in the circle.

One day Ronnie and another student had a

confrontation on the school bus over some re-mark interpreted as a racial slur. I went to the school to talk to him, and the principal, a skilled and compassionate man, met with us.

Ronnie stonewalled us with his inscrutable smile. He insisted that there was "no prob-lem." He had plenty of friends. In fact, every-body in the world was his friend. He recognized no problem in this incident nor in anything else going on in his life. He had no problem with white people except that they didn't like him, but that was no problem. He had no problem, period.

Finally, the principal looked him in the eye and said gently but firmly, "Ronnie, you sit alone in the cafeteria every day at lunch. You're alone at recess. You're 'off the wall' in the gifted program. How can you sit there and tell me that you have plenty of friends? Where are they?"

I also demanded that he look me in the eye.

"Ronnie, I'm white. Do I like you? Am I your friend? Mr. Marshall is black. He's your friend. Can you see that?"

He stared at me. After a long silence, I re-peated the question.

Slowly, reluctantly, he responded, "Yes, ma'am. You and Mr. Marshall do like me."

I persisted. "The students in our program. Do they like you?"

He thought it through. Finally he nodded his head.

"Yes, ma'am. They're my friends, too."

After that encounter, he "came alive" in the program. He even emerged as a leader in the group, probably the most respected member of his class.


No, I will not abandon you
or leave you as orphans in the storm—
I will come to you.

John 14:18 TLB


Lord, help me to see the lonely and aban-
    doned among us.
Let me care as You care, and befriend those
    whom You love.
Let me confront them when it's necessary,
    so that they can see what they have to see
    in order to survive.

# Broken–Down Walls
## 2 Peter 1:5–9

Like a city whose walls are broken down
is a man who lacks self-control.
                              Proverbs 25:28

He had a terrible temper. When he was angry, his temper quickly escalated out of control.

One day he and another student got into a violent disagreement. I had to separate them. Sam got away from me and ran across the school yard into the adjacent woods. The students and I went in search of him, and after a short time he came back, sullen and defiant.

Sam and I sat on the steps of the portable classroom and talked. I had called his mother, who said helplessly, "I can't do a thing with him when he gets like this. His father is the only one who can handle him, and he's out of town. Just do what you have to do."

I said to Sam, "I can take over and make you straighten out. That won't help you next time. You have to get control of this yourself. I'm going to leave you here to work this out by yourself. Let me know when you're ready to come back to the group."

He stayed apart through lunch (which I brought to him at his request) and into the afternoon. Finally, he sent for me.

"I still don't like him, but I can come back into the group and get along."

From that time on, Sam did not lose his temper in our group. He worked things out inside himself, taking control of his own reactions.

Better a patient man than a warrior,
a man who controls his temper than one
who takes a city.

Proverbs 16:32

If it is true that I have gone astray,
my error remains my concern
alone.

Job 19:4

Lord,
> You make me responsible for
> my own actions.
> You provide what I need to get into control.
> Forgive me when I forget.
> Forgive me when I fail to reach out for
> what is available to me.
> Thank You for Your patience with me.
> Give me Your patience for those who have
> trouble
> controlling their own behavior.

And, Lord,
> could You please show us what to do about
> the "broken–down walls"
> of authority all around us, especially
> in the homes where no one is in charge?
> Help us, Lord.

# Facing Finals
## Matthew 22:34–40

Aunt Marjory Langston taught me in the fourth grade. I couldn't bring myself to call her "Aunt Marjory" in the classroom, so I addressed her as "Teacher."

She lived ninety-two full years, and for all those years she was to me and to many other people, "Teacher." In the classroom, she definitely was of the "old school," requiring us to sit up straight, pay attention, and behave ourselves.

Not long before her death, I visited Aunt Marjory for yet another lesson. She always welcomed questions, so I asked her, "How would you sum up all that you have learned?"

She thought that over and, in her precise speech, said, "All it adds up to is love."

Aunt Marjory had been strict. She held high standards, lived up to those standards herself and expected others to do the same. But her entire life came to be summed up in love. Not only did she *say* it, she lived it. People called her on the telephone after she became limited in getting around, and she prayed with them. She cared about each of them.

Not long before Jesus, Master Teacher, died, a lawyer came up to Him, testing Him (a "final examination"?), and asked Him, in effect, What is the most important of all the vast lists of commandments written in the Torah?

Jesus looked him in the eye and stated, "Love God with your whole heart and your neighbor as yourself."

Aunt Marjory said, "All it adds up to is love."

That kind of love is tough. It cannot be learned in an overnight "cramming session." Learning any new concept takes, for the average intelligence, eight repetitions to fix it in the mind. To unlearn and relearn a concept ("reprogram a concept") requires sixty-four repetitions.

Love, to become truly learned and put into practice, must be experienced over and over again in caring actions. (Was this what Jesus taught Peter about forgiveness—seventy times seven repetitions to relearn a false concept about limited forgiveness? *See* Matthew 18:21, 22.)

God is Love.

God took action to rescue us.

So did Aunt Marjory. She cared enough to teach me for fifty years. And what she taught me, she learned from God.

Thank You, Father, for Aunt Marjory.
Thank You for each teacher who cared about a little child.
Thank You most of all that You teach me, and You never take a vacation from that instruction.
Please prepare me well for my "finals."

The path of the righteous is like the first gleam of dawn, shining ever brighter till the full light of day.

Proverbs 4:18

# How Will I Deal With This Clutter?
## Romans 8:28; Philippians 1:6

Now that the school year is ending, I am faced with accumulated clutter. I have to gather in rental books, clean out cabinets, store equipment, and leave the room prepared for a thorough summer cleaning.

I welcome this clearing out, but I don't know what to do with all the "loose ends." My own "stuff" is piled into boxes waiting to be organized. Maybe this summer I can actually go carefully through it all and get it perfectly ready for next year. I wonder how much of all of this is junk and how much is my teaching memory.

My friend lost eighteen years' accumulation of teaching materials in a fire that destroyed a wing of her school. How could I function without my own storehouse of "stuff"?

You must deal with a lot of loose ends, too, Lord. All around me I see beginnings but few "closures," and I wonder how neat and efficient You are, how carefully You tie things together. When I look back through my life, I see loose ends and I wonder what You're doing.

According to Romans 8:28, You waste nothing. Not even the hurtful things, the evil that we do, the mistakes we make—nothing is wasted in Your grand design. It excites me to glimpse this truth when I see You put together broken fragments and loose ends.

Recently I talked with a former student, now a deacon in his church. He said, "I was always quiet, but I did listen. As far as I was concerned, you and your husband [who was his pastor] were my connection to God."

I remember the effort I put into those students, the exhaustion, the discouragement, and the question—"Does any of it get through?"

As I listened to Danny, I knew in a flash that it *matters* to You what we do! What we give sincerely to You, even in our blundering way, You take seriously, and You meticulously

store it up to fit it into Your grand design. You
certainly don't operate on our time schedule.
You often don't move as quickly as we would
like, but You never waste one minute or one
gift given to You from our hearts.

Thank You, careful God,
     That You waste nothing given to You.
Thank You that You can take even our
     blunders,
        even our sins, truly repented of,
        and use them to teach us,
        to discipline us,
        to make us sensitive to those who hurt
        because they have failed.

He who began a good work in you will
carry it on to completion. . . .
                              Philippians 1:6

# "Commencing"—What?
## Colossians 1:9–11

Countless high school "commencements" bring families streaming into large arenas and small auditoriums to celebrate. Cameras flash as each "Class of 1991" marches across the stage to receive coveted diplomas. What do we want for them? What do they want for themselves?

One speaker urges "simplicity," in the spirit of Thoreau who entreated us to "simplify, simplify." How would Thoreau react to a fast-food age of acquisition when bumper stickers proclaim that "He who dies with the most toys—wins!"

Another voice talks of "truth," echoing Pilate, who asked Jesus, "What is truth?" Now a young man says, "I don't have any beliefs any-

more. All the arguing made me give up on
what I thought I believed." Has he given up
on the search for truth, or discarded outworn
and borrowed thinking?

These young people graduate from one
level of education and "commence" another
phase of learning. For them, the search for
knowledge has just begun, even though they
may not realize it yet. The search for wisdom
may not yet have awakened in their hearts.
Those who have taught them can only hope
that they have been given the tools by which
they will continue to increase in knowledge
and grow in wisdom.

The concept of "freedom" threads through
the speeches. Students see their "freedom"
just around the corner, and we have to ask
them, "Are you sure you're ready for that?" In
public speeches, *freedom* is usually linked with
responsibility, which equals "awareness" and
"challenge."

Grandparents look on these scenes with
fond approval, and parents watch with careful
eyes: Is his hair combed? Is her lipstick
smeared? Will they embarrass us or will they
make us proud? How do we cope with what
comes next? Can I let her go to First Week at
the beach? Should I have insisted on chaper-
oning her group?

Younger children, all dressed up, look at the pageantry and count the years before they get to walk across that stage. For each family, there is only *one* graduate, even through the relentless list of alphabetized names.

For the faculty of each school, it is the end of another bonding, as we ask ourselves, *What will next year's class be like?* for each class develops its own distinct personality and presents us with its own particular problems.

Our Father,
> May I never stop praying for these young
>     people,
> asking that You fill them with the knowl-
>     edge of Your will
> through all spiritual wisdom and
>     understanding,
> that they may live lives that bear fruit in
>     every good work,
> growing in the knowledge of God,
>     strengthened
> to endure with all patience,
>     joyfully giving thanks to
>     the Father.

∽

. . . With God all things are possible.
                    Matthew 19:26

# Free at Last!
## Psalm 62:5–8

The rhythm of the ocean waves reminds me of the rhythm of the school year. At times the sea lies placid and still, with gentle waves breaking almost imperceptibly along the shore beneath a cloudless blue sky. I catch my breath at the beauty of it, and forget the threat of storms.

At other times, the sky turns gray with an approaching storm, the wind quickens, the tide rushes in, and the waves swell, break, and crash violently against the sand barriers.

In such a sea, I don't dare to put more than a tentative foot into the surf because of the heavy pull of the undertow. But when the tide is right, I ride the waves, as they rise and fall in a relaxing pattern.

The crazy rhythm of the school year is over, all of it: the placid, sky blue days when my classes run smoothly and I can "go with the flow," and the turbulent days when nothing at all goes according to plan and I wish I could run away.

For these days at the beach I can take a break from routine, walk on hot sand, cool my feet in cool saltwater, and exult in the sweep of sky and sea, moving in its own order and control.

I believe this is what I like most about the beach: I do not have to decide the tides or control the waves. The sea creatures move about in ceaseless search for nourishment, and not one of them depends on me for anything. I do not have to ask questions or answer them.

After this short break, I will go home, to relish the summer weeks of hot sun and cool breezes, picnics in the park and cold drinks in an air-conditioned house. After these days away, I can face intervals of preparation for next year and begin to build excitement again for the shorter days of September when the tide turns and the waves again move toward the shore.

I am a teacher.

I am a teacher on summer vacation.
I am a teacher renewing her strength to begin again, come September.

Lord of all sand, and sea, and sky,
   Lord of all creation,
   Who separated the land from the water,
   and called it "good,"
Thank You for this Your creation,
   for sharing with us Your delight in
      soaring gulls
   and glistening fish, leaping in the
      sunlight,
Thank You that I, also, am Your creation,
   and You delight in me.

My Presence will go with you, and I will
      give you rest.
Exodus 33:14

# Bits and Pieces
# Jeremiah 18:1–6

In Charleston for the Spoleto Festival, I visited the "Disaster Museum" featuring artwork by students who had survived major disasters in 1989 (Charleston's Hurricane Hugo, the San Francisco earthquake, and Huntsville's tornado). On a tall stand stood a beautiful ceramic vase. Beneath it was this inscription:

> When the earthquake struck, everything in our house was broken, and my mom lost many beautiful treasures that had belonged to her mother. I saw how much she grieved over it, and I gathered up the broken pieces and decided to put them together. I thought it might make her feel worse, but she loves it.

Imbedded in the potter's material are bits of porcelain, a tiny doll's face, a bit of a dainty cup, each one a poignant reminder of a family treasure.

God has done that for me. The "earthquakes" of my life have destroyed things that I treasure, and I mourned each broken piece.

*But God*, when He saw my grief, tenderly took up the fragments and set them into the clay of my life, as He placed me on the potter's wheel and reshaped my future.

Recently I had lunch with a friend whose life fell apart this year. She struggles with the "what ifs" and the pain of regret. Her friends and her family are helping her gather up the precious and beautiful pieces of her life, and she is finding courage to let God reshape her future.

Not even an earthquake separated that San Francisco mother from her daughter's love and from the richness of their family heritage. Even so, no disaster can separate us from the love of God which is in Christ Jesus.


Loving Father,
> You see the devastation brought to
> Charleston by the
> force of the hurricane.

You see the brokenness in every place of
   physical disaster.
You see the inner brokenness in my
   friend, and her brave struggle to put
   her life back together.
Thank You that we do not struggle alone.
Thank You for time to share with each
   other and with You what it means to be
   broken, and what it means to be
   repaired.

For I am convinced that neither death nor
life . . . nor anything else in all creation,
will be able to separate us from the love
of God
that is in Christ Jesus our Lord.
                         Romans 8:38, 39

# "It Took a Man to Hit My Heart"
## Isaiah 61:1–3

After a trip to Washington with his eighth-grade class, Chip Thornton described some "very memorable things," but the one that impressed him most was a young "entertainer" in the courtyard in front of the White House.

This young dancer "seemed to be in his early thirties, and probably hadn't been sober in a week. He had a stocking cap over his eyes and dirty clothes on. He danced around a statue of Andrew Jackson in some kind of ritual movement which probably dated back to medieval times. It was awfully funny until it hit me. . . . The sight of that man made me realize that our country isn't in such a great financial 'plus.'

"Although we saw many . . . monuments, it

took a man to hit my heart and open my eyes to the real world. Monuments do not make up the country, people do. Why can't we restore them?"

This young student "hits my heart" as I think of our country and its heritage on this Independence Day celebrating our freedom. Those who died in the wars of our country died to guarantee the freedom of that young derelict to dance his drunken dance in front of the president's home.

Chip asks a good question: Why can't we restore the people of our country? Why must there be drunkenness and poverty? Why must there be hopelessness and despair? In a land of incredible resources, why is there so much pain?

Chip himself, and the other students who banded together on an unforgettable trip to our nation's capital, are a ray of hope for our country. They will become our leaders; as they understand our history and face our problems, they will seek out solutions we have not found.

Do they know what the "good news" is?

Do they accept their freedom—with responsibility?

Do they seek their own good, or the anointing of God to bring good news to the poor?

We not only face physical poverty, but also a poverty of spirit, in the brokenness of violence and addiction.

Jesus died to accomplish a specific mission summed up in Isaiah 61:1–3: "to bestow . . . a garment of praise instead of a spirit of despair."

Thank You, God,
    for the teachers who made it possible
      for Chip to go to Washington.
Thank You that his eyes were wide open to
        what he saw.
Grant that we may catch his vision,
and exercise our freedom with responsibility,
so that the people of our country may be
        restored.

# Harmonic Interludes
## Psalm 42:5, 11; 43:5

At lunch last week, a friend said, "I'm so glad summer is here! By the end of the year I always begin to feel like a robot, programmed to do my job. It takes the summer break to make me spiritual again."

Tuning in to the life of the spirit is much easier in the cool, hushed, and responsive atmosphere of a chamber music concert at historic Dock Street Theatre in Charleston than it is in a crowded, noisy school cafeteria! Even during the concert, my "teacher's mind" replays unanswered questions from the school year.

Robert Schumann is described as a "classic manic-depressive, with suicide never far from his mind." In the haunting beauty of his music, he reveals this troubled state of mind with brilliant intensity and vivid harmonic changes.

In his "Three Romances for Oboe and Piano" Schumann's melody repeats over and over a cry, a question, a plea that finds no real response, but eventually a resolution into acceptance, for now, of that pain which could not be completely eradicated.

I also heard a young Israeli pianist play a Bach toccata, with its simple statement of a melodic theme continuing in more and more intricate patterns as other simple themes were introduced, until the effect became overpowering in its force and intensity.

Summer can become for me a "spiritual interlude" when the simple themes that have built up in my life can achieve harmony and blend into a full and satisfying completion.

Three times in two psalms, one of the "sweet singers of Israel" asked repeatedly, "Why are you downcast, O my soul?" The psalms give us the source of that harmony: Hope in God, for I will yet praise Him.

Listening to Schumann's music, or, even better, playing it on the piano, satisfies the moods within my own spirit. He found release for his troubled tendencies through his music, and left it as a legacy for others to find their own release.

So God uses each of us as His channels to unlock His flow of energy and love, each in the expression of that unique gift of personality and the combination of talents that He has placed within us.

In the intricacies of music, we trust the master composers for a satisfying resolution. Even so, we hope in the Lord our God to bring into our lives His own completion.

Oh, God,
    In the complex melodies of my life
  may I distinguish the crystal clarity of Your
              Word
  speaking again its pure truth to my heart:
God is love, and he who dwells in love dwells
            in God.

# Sand Sculptures
## 1 Corinthians 3:5–15

Walking along the shore in the late afternoon, we pass sand sculptures carefully or casually constructed during the day when the tide is out. As the tide turns, the waves lap against the sand, quickly erasing all traces of the designs.

In a large shopping mall in Chattanooga I saw a huge, elaborate sand sculpture depicting phases of the history and geography of the state of Tennessee. Molded only of sand and water, the figures brought alive the natural phenomena of beavers building a dam, mountains and trees, two men rafting down the rivers. The artists also reconstructed a medieval castle on the top of a mountain, which contrasted sharply with the miners' cabins hugging the side of a steep trail, and a train emerging from a tunnel.

The details of the sculpture astonished me. Even though an explanatory note stated that the sculpture would "last almost indefinitely" inside, away from any effects of erosion, eventually the mall will change its display and the elaborate artwork will be scooped up into piles of sand and carted off for the artists to begin again, in yet another temporary location.

I could not help asking myself how these men feel when their work is torn down repeatedly. Would they not prefer to give their lives to something more permanent?

How about me? What am I giving my life to construct?

Certainly in education we never see a "finished product," but it is encouraging to see long-term results. When I visited St. Phillip's Church in Charleston, I saw among the pictures of their staff one of my former students, and I remembered the way his life had been shaped in the seventh grade. It is encouraging when successful students come back into our lives and reassure us that our influence meant something, after all.

When we recognize that we are not responsible for the "grand design," we can fit into

"God's architecture" and go about serenely shaping our sand sculptures under His direction, knowing that the permanence lies in our obedience, not in the closure we may or may not see.

*Isn't it strange that princes and kings*
*And clowns that caper in sawdust rings*
*And common folks like you and me*
*Are builders for eternity?*

*To each is given a bag of tools,*
*A shapeless mass, and a bag of rules*
*And each must build ere life has flown*
*A stumbling block or a stepping stone.*

Anonymous

## Silent Witnesses
## Hebrews 12:1–3

Dappled sunlight falls across the mountains, highlighting lush summer foliage in all shades of green, from palest young leaves to the deep, rich, dark hues of cone-shaped cedars and spruce.

Down the side of a mountain a clean swath of rock separates the rich vegetation. On the other side of the highway, layers of slate reveal the violent ruptures where the smoothly graded interstate has cut through the forbidding landscape. Signs warn of falling rocks caused by the unsettling invasion of technology.

I think of those who walked through virgin forests exploring new territory, seeking worn footpaths and never dreaming of graded interstates teeming with cars from all over the continent and huge trucks lumbering up the sides of impossible mountains.

The pioneers walked, not so long ago compared to the age of the hills, and a little later they rode in rough wagons pulled by laboring beasts of burden. The bodies of man and beast lie now in unmarked graves scattered across the country, and we ride uncaring over their tortuous and now obliterated paths.

What would they say to us, this great cloud of witnesses, about our interstates and our fast cars and huge trucks? Would they mourn their forests or would they join us gleefully on the interstate and set off to see the country?

Grandpa Booth sat on the porch of his farmhouse ten miles from town and marveled at the occasional car that stirred up dust on the unpaved road.

"People do ride!" he exclaimed in wonder.

I hear him when I watch the ceaseless traffic or face cars backed up for miles because of an accident ahead. Where could all these people be going?

I must prepare students to become the engineers of the future, to design the roads, but also to construct the roads with hot tar in burning sunlight. Can I respect those who follow and obey as well as those who design and lead others?

Will I be proud if one of my students becomes president and recognizes me in the Inauguration Ceremony? Will I be equally proud if one of my students teaches my grandchildren?

Lord,
    you have been our dwelling place
       throughout all generations.
    Before the mountains were born
    or you brought forth the earth
       and the world
    from everlasting to everlasting
       you are God. . . .
    Establish the work of our
       hands for us—
    yes, establish the work of
       our hands.
                 Psalm 90:1, 2, 17

# Don't They Know This Is My Vacation?
## Matthew 16:24–26

Lord, I thought I'd get by this summer without helping out in Vacation Bible School. I had asked to be relieved of that responsibility, because I really think I need a break from teaching during the summer months. After I work with students all the rest of the year, I can't be too cheerful about adding another week or two in the summer, with all the planning and preparation that goes into it.

They did apologize, but then they added what they always say, "It's so easy for you, since you know how to teach. After all, you do this all the time!"

That's just the point, Lord. I do this all the time. Am I not entitled to some time off?

Interesting word, *entitled*. What *am* I entitled to? What do I deserve, anyway?

A cross, You said.

Take up my cross and follow You.

What is my cross?

I've often had a sneaking notion that my "cross" was any disagreeable thing You made me do, even though I didn't want to do it. Taking it up made me feel like a martyr, and that affected my disposition—negatively, I might add.

Shall I play the martyr and work in Bible school?

For some later reward, perhaps?

I can talk myself into it, by remembering the good times and the positive experiences I have had with the children in Bible school. I can do my duty and feel good about it. After all, there will be time to rest up before school starts again.

Is this all my obedience amounts to? Is this worth calling a "cross"?

Does it matter whether or not we have Bible school?

Does it matter that the children learn Your Word?

Does it matter that we have trained people to teach them?

I see little Cliff's face as he runs in from his class to show his mama what he made in Bible school, and I thank You that his teacher cared enough to plan that lesson.

Does it matter that other people taught me?

It matters, Lord. It matters a lot.

Forgive my fleeting reluctance.

Forgive my persistent self-interest.

Stir me up with the energy only You can give.

Fire my imagination with Your own creative mind, and flood my body with the "strength of ten"!

∽

. . . whatever you did
for one of the least of these brothers of
mine, you did for me.

Matthew 25:40

# Where Did the Summer Go?
# Matthew 13:52

I know it's August when . . .
>the days suddenly grow shorter
>the heat lingers all night long
>the stores fill up with school supplies
>and a letter comes telling me about
>>in-service.

My house is clean,
>the closets have been organized,
>the stacked-up books have been read,
>the summer clothes look jaded,
>and I wonder if my classroom is ready
>>yet.

My cup of summer is full and running over,
>and I am ready now to experiment
>with new plans, new students,
>a fresh environment.

I believe I'll borrow an idea from a friend of mine and gift wrap a small square of Styrofoam to place on each student's desk, and tell them,

"This represents your 'gift,' which we will discover during this year together. I might see these gifts on the floor or in the trash can, or perhaps I will see them appear on my desk at the end of the year. Will the gift be realized during this year? I hope so."

I am eager to go into my "storehouse" of ideas and bring out "new treasures" as well as old.

I might even tell them the story of the boy who visited Stone Mountain and watched a sculptor with a chisel, working on a piece of rock. A year later, he returned, and saw to his astonishment the nearly completed figure of a lion where the rock had been.

The little boy asked the sculptor, "How did you know that lion was in there?"

Lord,
  Let me see the "lion" inside every student
    I meet in my classroom this year.
  Steady my hands as I carve out the image
    of what each one can become.

May I never glory in my wisdom or
strength, but in this,
that I understand and know Him
who is my God.
                    *See* Jeremiah 9:23, 24